Other books by Barbara Jurgensen:

How to Live Better on Less

A Polluter's Garden of Verses

Leaping Upon the Mountains

All the Bandits of China

Oh, Please . . . Not Bethlehem!

Men Who Dared

Parents, Ugh

Quit Bugging Me

The Lord Is My Shepherd, But

You're Out of Date, God

Don't Bug Me, Preacher

Some Day We've Got to Get Organized

God Probably Doesn't Know I Exist

The
Prophets
Speak
Again

A Brief
Introduction
to
Old Testament
Prophecy

The Prophets Speak Again

BARBARA JURGENSEN

AUGSBURG PUBLISHING HOUSE
MINNEAPOLIS, MINNESOTA

Copyright © 1977 Augsburg Publishing House

Library of Congress Catalog Card No. 76-27084

International Standard Book No. 0-8066-1566-4

Scripture quotations unless otherwise noted are from the Revised Standard Version of the Bible, copyright 1946, 1952, and 1971 by the Division of Christian Education of the National Council of Churches.

Manufactured in the United States of America.

Contents

Preface

I have tried to listen in on the prophets as they spoke to their people and to their God. Sometimes they shouted and shook their fists; sometimes they spoke so softly that one almost had to stop breathing to hear them. When I have quoted their words exactly from the Revised Standard Version, the chapter and verse numbers are cited.

Who Were
the Prophets?

The prophets were people. Not angels. Not super-beings. Not some strange kind of creatures. People.

People who lived God's way in troubled and difficult times.

People who dared, in the midst of a hostile world, to stand up for God.

People who uttered God's words as he gave them, regardless of threats to their own lives.

The secret of their courage and endurance? They knew God. For them God was not some shadowy, faraway, unknowable being. He was knowable and near. They knew him not only from their study of the Scriptures; they had gone on to know him personally, pondering his Word and talking to him as they went about their daily lives.

The prophets were people endowed with the same potential the rest of us are endowed with —the potential of becoming the people of God. Their prophecies usually concerned what was going to happen *if* people did not change their ways. Sometimes the people listened and changed and the predicted disasters did not need to happen. But more often the people went on as they had, and the disasters came.

Each prophet was different. Each had his own personality. Some were married and had families to support. For most of them, prophesying was not a profession but something they did in addition to regular work. It was payment enough to them that God had chosen them as a means of speaking to his people. So they went and declared God's words.

Each prophet had a particular message for the people of his time. Sometimes the prophets seem to us to be repeating each other, but we forget they were strung across history over some four or five hundred years and lived in various parts of the country. God called them into service whenever the people had slipped so far away that he needed some direct means of calling them back.

The prophets also prepared the way for Jesus. Had Jesus been born in Athens or Rome, the people in those cities probably would not have been ready to understand and receive him and his teachings. But coming as he did where prophets had gradually been leading the people into a more mature relationship with God, he found many who were eager and responsive.

The Hebrew prophets were unique among prophets of the world. The oracles at Delphi, the readers of animal entrails in Mesopotamia, and the augurs in Rome claimed to foretell the future, but only the Hebrew prophets claimed to speak the will of God.

The Hebrew prophets alone attempted to answer the riddle of life by showing people what their relationship to God and to their fellow human beings was to be. They showed the devastating effect of sin on a person's and a nation's life. They showed also that, as a person lives in a relationship of love to God and to fellow human beings, life becomes not only bearable, but meaningful and satisfying.

If these people, these prophets, were able to accomplish so much, why doesn't God send prophets today? Perhaps because he expects each Christian to bear his message. Perhaps because when he sent Christ he gave his full and complete word. In Christ he said and did all that needed to be said and done.

What Sort
of Person
Was a Prophet?

The prophet was a person who was overwhelmed by the glory and the presence of God. Amos wrote,

> He who forms the mountains, and creates the wind,
>   and declares to man what is his thought;
> who makes the morning darkness,
>   and treads on the heights of the earth—
> the Lord, the God of hosts, is his name! (4:13).

While others harkened to sounds of the world, the prophet heard God speaking in a still, small voice or roaring from the top of Mt. Zion. But mostly he heard God communicating with him in his heart, urging him to call his people back.

The prophet had an overpowering sense of the otherness, the holiness of God; he was intoxicated by God's greatness. Yet he also knew that this almighty one continued to reach out in concern to guide his children.

Therefore the prophet saw sin as a cosmic disorder rupturing a person's harmony with himself, with others, and with his Creator. He refused to accept sin as the normal state of life. He did not propose social, political, or economic reforms. Instead he called his people back to their covenant relationship with God, that they would be God's people and he would be their God.

But the prophet knew this relationship had to be more than a security blanket. God was calling men and women to step off the meaningless treadmill of the world to a new life. God was calling individuals into his kingdom.

So, while those around him slept, the prophet heard the voice of God thundering from heaven, calling him to awaken the people. Rising up, he tried to tell the people what God had said so plainly to him, but they rarely were interested. He tried to enflame their hearts with the words that had blazed their way into his, but their hearts were fire-resistant.

The word of God, so clear to him, was meaningless to them. He heard God shaking the very foundations of the universe; they heard nothing.

The people tolerated each prophet for a while, until the novelty and entertainment value wore off. Then people began to realize he was talking about life and death matters and calling on them to make choices, to live as mature people, and they decided to lock him up in the village stocks or throw him into a musty jail cell or chase him out of town.

Even more, they began to realize that if they did not heed the prophet's words, disaster for the whole nation could result. Their dislike for him turned to fear and hate. The man who had been chosen by God was now rejected by his people. Some prophets were stoned.

So a prophet had to be willing to suffer. Speaking for God was not a hobby he practiced on alternate weekends if the weather was clement. His whole being had to be dedicated or he could not have carried through. A prophet chose to put not only his voice but his whole person into God's service.

A prophet therefore could be very lonely. No wonder he often poured out his anguish to God.

But there was also the other side to the vocation; being a conveyor of God's word could bring great joy. Though all people seemed to be against him at times, he knew the exhilaration and peace of living as God's person. By placing himself in God's employ, he exposed himself more seriously to God's chastisement, but also to his life-giving presence.

God never leaves himself without a witness; he always has those who are living out his purposes in the world. So none of his lessons are wasted, he always works through chosen servants, making his way known to the world. Amos wrote that the Lord does nothing without revealing his secret to his servants the prophets, so dwellers of the earth may see, whether they choose to or not, that God is working out his purposes.

While others are mired in the here and now, the prophet ascends the mountain for a view, not only of the past and the present, but of the future. He sees spread out in vast panorama God's concern for all peoples. Humbly he listens, then goes back down to deliver the message.

Some have called the prophet the first universal human being; others, God's ambassador at large. Most prophets would have preferred to be known simply as one of the people of God.

How Did God Guide the Prophets?

The prophet was definitely not a mere tape recorder for God. God selected a person willing to serve him with his heart, soul, and mind. Now and then a prophet became weary of his role. Some even ran in the opposite direction, as did Jonah. But in the main the prophets were willing to put their whole lives into God's service.

God spoke to the chosen person in dreams or visions or thoughts or through everyday events. However he chose to reveal his message, God made it plain to his prophet that this was a word from the Lord of all creation, a word he must pass on to his people.

Unlike the ambassador of a nation, who needs to maintain a degree of detachment, the prophet needed to be completely involved with the message he was to communicate. Once he received it, he turned it over in his mind, molding it into a form that would best speak to the people of his day. For this reason no two prophets delivered their message in exactly the same way. Some were very straightforward; others used poetic language. Some tried to reason with their people; others simply passed on the message to them. Whatever way they chose, they were used by God to the full extent of their human capabilities to convey his message.

The prophet shared the very heart of God. God revealed to the prophet his thoughts and intentions, his concerns and plans for the future. Then God left it up to him to put these across to the people (perhaps guiding and restraining him, pulling him back and pushing him forward as needed).

At times God had his prophets perform symbolic acts to put his message across in the most forceful way possible, as when he told Jeremiah to wear a yoke of wood to symbolize the bondage that would soon come upon his people. They would soon put their necks under the yoke of Nebuchadnezzar, king of Babylon.

These symbolic acts were an intensified form of prophetic speech. Sometimes their meaning was not disclosed to the people until years later (as when Isaiah walked naked and barefoot among his people). Some prophecies were to be sealed up until a later time or even until the last days (as in the case of Daniel).

So God laid a burden on his prophets, weighing them down with the heaviness of the message until they could find peace only in passing it on to their people.

Each day God guided his prophets, opening their eyes to the misery of the mistreated, the plight of the poor. Each day he helped them feel the pain of the downtrodden as God himself felt it, to see the wrongdoing of the people as it was seen by God himself, to hear the voice of God calling the people to be his once more.

So the prophet became a person with fierce emotions. While others muddled along with a sense of cosmic aloneness and purposelessness, the prophet was overwhelmed by God's presence and by his own effort to communicate this presence to his people.

It was embarrassing and distressing at times to be God's prophet. False prophets offered soothing words to the people while he, the true prophet, had to predict pestilence, agony, and destruction. It could be a lonely job. The prophet was often mocked. "I spend my days in shame," wrote Jeremiah (20:18).

Yet God promised to be with his prophets. "You shall be as my mouth," he said to Jeremiah; "I am with you to save you and deliver you" (15:19-20). And there were times of great joy. "Thy words became to me a joy and a delight of my heart," wrote Jeremiah, "for I am called by thy name, O Lord, God of hosts" (15:16).

The prophets knew their strength was from God. They had lived in his presence long enough and gone through enough difficult times with him to be willing to trust him, even when he led them by strange and terrifying paths.

Above all, the prophets had the satisfaction of carrying God's word to his people, for the very Lord of the universe had said to them, as he said to Ezekiel:

> I send you to the people of Israel, to a nation of rebels, who have rebelled against me; they and their fathers have transgressed against me to this very day. The people also are impudent and stubborn: I send you to them; and you shall say to them, 'Thus says the Lord God.' And whether they hear or refuse to hear (for they are a rebellious house) they will know that there has been a prophet among them (2:3-5).

What Did
the Prophets Do?

The Hebrew prophet saw God not as an idea but as a person. For the prophets the whole earth was full of his glory, and they found their lives' meaning in living in his presence, in putting their abilities into his service.

For them faith was more than agreeing to believe a set of teachings; it was knowing the God of all creation as their Lord. How could other people fail to see his majesty wherever they looked? How could they not see his hand at work in the world?

In response to this God, who was as real to them as their neighbors, the prophets witnessed to his mercy, his justice, and his judgment. They were his messengers, his watchmen, his defenders, his servants, his representatives to and for his people.

They knew the people they lived among and they knew the God who lived among them, and they walked in compassion with both.

But the prophets were not utopians. They had no optimism about human institutions. If better days were to come, they knew they would be by God's doing, not man's. They knew some things are beyond human power. People, they said, have choice but not sovereignty, and when they try to shape history in disregard and defiance of God, disaster will result.

The predominant method of the prophets was exhortation, challenging the emptiness of the people's religion, scuttling their illusions of security, throwing down their sacred icons so God could be put in the center again. Standing up against priest and king when necessary, they declared what would happen if the people kept on as they were. Their fundamental objective: to reconcile God and his people.

The prophets differed greatly from moralists and from the seers of other religions. Moralists want people to improve their ways; the prophets wanted people to enter into a whole new relationship with the very Lord of the universe. The seers of other religions tried to satisfy their constituents' desire to see into the future with visions of good days to come; the prophets tried to shock their people into making changes by describing disastrous days to come if they continued in their faithless way.

The prophets claimed attention for no other reason than that they spoke in the name of the Lord. True, they had turned the powers of their minds toward understanding God and his ways. But their messages were not from their thoughts, but the word of God.

The major role of the prophets then was interference. With stern words, they pronounced doom upon their people. But these words were followed by a message of hope and redemption, by the promise that in returning to God their people would find reconciliation and life itself.

In the presence of God the prophets took the part of the people; in the presence of the people, the part of God. Their lives were lived between the two, interpreting God's ways to their people, pleading with God to ease up and give the people one more chance.

So every prediction of disaster became an exhortation to repentance. Impatient with their people's excuses and disdainful of their pretense and self-pity, the prophets attacked with slashing words to try to bring them to a responsible relationship with God.

It is surprising that the prophets were tolerated at all. The pious found them blasphemous in their claims to be speaking for God; those in authority found them a threat to the nation's security in their admonitions to yield to enemy forces; those who had lapsed from the faith found them not only a nuisance but infuriating. Amos wrote, "They abhor him who speaks the truth" (5:10).

If the people hadn't realized somewhere back in the dim recesses of their minds that the prophets' words were of ultimate concern, they probably would have subjected them to even more laughter, beatings, and stonings.

The prophets kept on, aware that if they did not proclaim the message God had given them to deliver they could be responsible for the downfall of their people. Often their mission was as repugnant to them as it was to their hearers. It was not pleasant to have to go before one's own people and tell them they were bringing disaster upon themselves. Nor was any reward promised the prophet if he succeeded, except that of having served his people and his God.

Why Did God
Send the Prophets?

God is at work in the world, building his kingdom, gathering his people. Beginning long ago with Abraham and Isaac and Jacob and the resulting nation of Israel, he has tried to bring his creatures out of their callousness into a life-giving relationship with him, with themselves, and with their fellow human beings.

To do all this, he started out with one nation. He planted a vineyard in Israel, but it yielded sour grapes. He sought to raise up a people who would understand and live by ways that bring life, but they preferred ways of injustice.

God sent the prophets to call his people back. Early in Israel's life the prophets began tending this vineyard, shaping the branches and pruning them back when necessary.

The people little appreciated being shaped and pruned, but God kept right on sending the prophets to perform his righteous task.

Right and wrong are not simply options for daily conduct. They shape the dimensions of world history. God's commandments are not mere recommendations. In the end justice will not fail; God will require an accounting of each person. Concern for the world is the very being of God. When his people grow callous, he cannot keep silent.

So God sent his prophets to help his people understand what he required, to help them get things in perspective. Throughout history people have sought happiness through leading selfish lives. Selfishness can only lead to misery, but because it is universal, it doesn't seem a problem. Rather than confess selfishness and seek help, people harden their hearts.

At this point God often steps into an individual's or a nation's life. When his people would harden their hearts, determined to continue their selfish ways, he would raise up a prophet to show them both what their problem was and the way out of it.

God entrusted his words to a long line of prophets stretching from Abraham through Moses, Samuel, Elijah, Isaiah, and on down to Malachi. This chain of communication, extending over many centuries, is unparalleled in human history. Through the prophets, the God who keeps himself from human gaze briefly pulled back the curtain.

Never has God given up on his people. He shapes and prunes his vineyard, that it may thrive and be more fruitful. Instead of pampering his people, he makes demands on them, that they may flourish and make his way known in the world.

The non-Israelites of Canaan and other countries of the Ancient Near East looked to their gods primarily for one thing: to provide what was necessary to sustain life. But the God of Israel wanted his people (and through them all people on earth) to become full human beings, a community of redeemed and redeeming people.

Therefore the God of Israel continually reached out to his people, motivated by love, but with judgment when necessary. His judgment demonstrated conclusively that he is the Lord of all and none is like him.

The prophets proclaimed ahead of time that a particular disaster would strike if the people continued as they were. If they didn't change their ways beforehand, at least the people could look back afterwards and realize that God demands truth and justice. He loves his people with an everlasting love, but he will not let them turn aside forever.

As the book of Hosea says, God has smitten his

people that he may heal them. He has stricken them, but he will bind them up. His judgment is always conditional: if his people turn from sin, he will not smite them.

God is not selfish. He wants people to follow his ways, not for his sake, but for theirs. Those who follow his ways shall know life.

Isaiah

The Light That
Has Already Shined

About the year 740 B.C., the prophet Isaiah had a
vision of the Lord sitting on his throne in the
temple, high and lifted up. Above the throne
hovered the seraphim, angelic creatures with six
wings, who called to each other: "Holy, holy, holy
is the Lord of hosts; the whole earth is full of his
glory" (6:3).

At this the foundations of the temple shook and
the building was filled with smoke. Isaiah shud-
dered at this great display of splendor. "Woe is
me!" he said. "I am a man of unclean lips, and I
dwell in the midst of a people of unclean lips; for
my eyes have seen the King, the Lord of hosts!"
(6:5).

Then one of the seraphim flew to him with a

burning coal from the altar. Touching Isaiah's mouth with it, he said, "Your guilt is taken away, and your sin forgiven" (6:7).

God had a message to send to his people. Isaiah heard the voice of the Lord saying, "Whom shall I send, and who will go for us?" (6:8).

Immediately Isaiah answered, "Here am I! Send me!" (6:8).

God commanded Isaiah to go and speak to his people. He also warned Isaiah that the people's hearts had become so hardened that his words would fall on deaf ears.

God apparently finds it difficult to communicate with people who are unconcerned about the most important things in life. Perhaps he thought, "I wish they were either hot or cold. Then I could talk with them. This in-between, don't-care attitude makes it almost impossible." So he warned Isaiah that to help the people see themselves as they really were, he was going to "make the heart of this people fat, and their ears heavy, and shut their eyes'" (6:10).

Isaiah was greatly disturbed by this. "How long, O Lord?" he asked (6:11).

God's answer was anything but comforting: "Until cities lie waste without inhabitant, and houses without men," until the people are exiles in a foreign land (6:11).

Then through his prophet Isaiah God told his people a story about a man who "had a vineyard on a very fertile hill. He digged it and cleared it of stones, and planted it with choice vines; he built a watchtower in the midst of it, and hewed out a wine vat in it; and he looked for it to yield grapes, but it yielded wild grapes" (5:1-3).

Then God asked the people of Jerusalem and Judah to serve for a moment as judge and jury. "What more was there to do for my vineyard, that I have not done in it? When I looked for it to yield grapes, why did it yield wild grapes?" (5:4).

Without waiting for the people to answer, he went on to pronounce the verdict: "The vineyard of the Lord of hosts is the house of Israel" (5:7).

"And now I will tell you what I will do to my vineyard. I will remove its hedge and it shall be devoured; I will break down its wall, and it shall be trampled down; I will make it waste; it shall not be pruned or hoed, and briers and thorns shall grow up; I will also command the clouds that they rain no rain upon it" (5:5-6).

The Lord had still more to say: My people "have rejected the law of the Lord of hosts, and have despised the word of the Holy One of Israel. Therefore I will raise a signal for a nation afar off and speedily it comes! Their arrows are sharp, all their bows bent. Their roaring is like a lion. They growl and seize their prey, they carry it off, and none can rescue" (from 5:24-29).

The people would be taken into exile. But God also promised that when they had learned to trust him once more, they would be returned to their own land.

God sent a message through Isaiah about the role he had planned for his people Israel. He described the Messiah who was to come, the suffering Servant:

> I have put my Spirit upon him,
>> he will bring forth justice to the nations (42:1).
>
> He was oppressed, and he was afflicted, . . .
>> he was cut off out of the land of the living,
>> stricken for the transgression of my people
>> (53:7-8).
>
> I have given you as . . . a light to the nations,
>> to open the eyes that are blind,
>> to bring out the prisoners from the dungeon,
>> from the prison those who sit in darkness (42:6).
>
> All flesh shall know
>> that I am the Lord your Savior,
>> and your Redeemer, the Mighty One of Jacob
>> (49:26).

Many years from this time Jesus would stand up in the synagogue in his home town of Nazareth and read from Isaiah's writings:

> The Spirit of the Lord God is upon me,
>> because the Lord has anointed me
> to bring good tidings to the afflicted;
>> he has sent me to bind up the brokenhearted,
> to proclaim liberty to the captives,
>> and the opening of the prison
> to those who are bound (61:1).

After Isaiah warned God's people, the Assyrian army made repeated forays into the land of Palestine, carrying off captives from the northern part of the country and threatening the southern part around Jerusalem.

Then the Babylonians defeated the Assyrians and became masters of Palestine. Besieging the city of Jerusalem, they broke their way in and destroyed its homes, its protective walls, and its temple, and carried away many of the people to serve them in their capital city, Babylon.

There the people of Israel languished, lamenting their fate. They felt lonely, cut off from their homes, their temple, and their God. Life became dark indeed.

Many decades later, when the Persians conquered Babylon, they allowed God's people to return to their land and begin rebuilding their homes, their temple, and the wall around the city of Jerusalem.

God's people went from hardhearted and arrogant sinners to dispirited exiles in a strange land to followers once more of the God of all creation. They learned that the world is in God's hands. They came to realize once more that it was good to be God's people.

When Isaiah first spoke to them, they were still going through the motions of worshiping in the temple, but it meant little to them. As exiles in Babylon they began to understand worship as wholehearted response to the God who created and redeemed them and who sought communication with them. They returned to their homeland more open to this relationship.

After the dark years of invasion and exile they were ready to appreciate Isaiah's words about the coming Savior:

> The people who walked in darkness
>   have seen a great light;
> those who dwelt in a land of deep darkness,
>   on them has light shined.
> They rejoice before thee.
> For the yoke of his burden,
>   and the staff of his oppressor,
>   thou hast broken.
> For to us a child is born,
>   to us a son is given;
> and the government will be upon his shoulder,
>   and his name will be called
> "Wonderful Counselor, Mighty God,
>   Everlasting Father, Prince of Peace."
> Of the increase of his government and of peace
>   there will be no end,
> upon the throne of David, and over his kingdom,
>   to establish it, and to uphold it
> with justice and with righteousness
>   from this time forth and for evermore
>   (from 9:2-7).

After years in exile when they felt cut adrift from all purpose and meaning to life, God's people were ready to appreciate the coming kingdom of God that Isaiah spoke of:

> It shall come to pass in the latter days
>   that the mountain of the house of the Lord
> shall be established as the highest of the mountains,
>   and shall be raised above the hills;
> and all the nations shall flow to it,
>   and many peoples shall come, and say:

"Come, let us go up to the mountain of the Lord,
    to the house of the God of Jacob;
that he may teach us his ways
    and that we may walk in his paths."
For out of Zion shall go forth the law,
    and the word of the Lord from Jerusalem.
He shall judge between the nations,
    and shall decide for many peoples;
and they shall beat their swords into plowshares,
    and their spears into pruning hooks;
nation shall not lift up sword against nation,
    neither shall they learn war any more (2:2-4).

Through all Isaiah's words shine his awe and love for the one who reaches out to speak to his people, who provides salvation in one who came to earth as a child.

Isaiah saw not only the people's hard hearts, but also the unquenchable love of God. He saw not only the numbered days of earthly kingdoms, but also the kingdom of the Lord that shall have no end. He saw that even for those who sit in deepest darkness, the light has shined.

Isaiah looked forward to the day when Jesus, the suffering Servant, would come to lead God's people out of their darkness and into his light; out of their oppressing and being oppressed into his way of peace; out of their meaninglessness and into his kingdom.

The Book of Isaiah

Theme: Arise, shine; for your light has come.

Part I (1–39)

   A. God's people have rebelled against him, and he will humble them (1–12).

   B. God will also humble other nations (13–23).

   C. God will bring judgment upon all people in the last days (24–27).

   D. Therefore his people should trust him (28–39).

Part II (40–66)

   A. God is the Lord of nature and history (40–48).

   B. He will redeem his people through his suffering Servant (49-55).

   C. He will keep his promises (56–59).

   D. He calls all to be his people (60–66).

Jeremiah

The Prophet
Who Was Kidnapped

The people of Jeremiah's day had become so greedy and hardhearted that even when they were weighing out grain to sell to a widow they would slyly slip a rock among the kernels. So God said to Jeremiah, "Run through the streets of Jerusalem, and if you can find even one person who does justly, I will pardon the city."

Jeremiah went up and down the streets, looking everywhere, but could only find people stealing from their neighbors, overcharging the elderly, taking advantage of the poor and worshiping idols of wood and stone.

"How can you live this way?" Jeremiah asked the people. "How can you forget the covenant our ancestors made so long ago with God? The covenant said that we would be his people and he would be our God."

But no one paid any attention to him.

Then God said, "Tell the people that their enemies the Babylonians are beginning to march toward Jerusalem. If my people change their ways, I will spare them. If not, I will let the Babylonians come in like a boiling pot out of the north and completely overthrow them."

Still no one paid any attention.

Then Jeremiah tried speaking God's words to the people from the place where they would be most likely to listen, the steps of the temple. "How can you lie, cheat, steal, and worship all sorts of idols which don't even have as much power as a scarecrow in a cucumber field, then come into God's house as though you had done no wrong? You have made God's house a den of robbers. And you priests aren't speaking the truth to the people. You tell them there will be peace, but there can be no peace when people live wrongly. Therefore God says that he will destroy this temple and the city around it."

The people and priests listened for a few minutes, then decided they'd heard enough, and the order was given that Jeremiah was to speak no more from the temple.

The army of Babylon was marching steadily onward toward Jerusalem.

Then God told Jeremiah to go down to the potter's house. The prophet watched the potter take a large lump of moist clay, throw it onto the wheel, and shape it with his hands. When the potter saw that the pot was not going to be right, he pressed the clay back together into a lump and began fashioning a new pot from it.

Then God said to Jeremiah, "I can do the same thing to my people if they insist on doing evil. I am the potter, they are the clay." But again the people refused to hear.

Then God sent Jeremiah to purchase an old earthen jug and take some of the elders and priests out to a nearby valley. Holding the jug aloft in his hands, Jeremiah said to them, "The people are now past the stage of being reshaped. They are like this old, worthless jug, fit only to be discarded." Then he dashed the jug to the ground, and it broke into many pieces. "God says, 'Unless my people change their ways, in the same way I will completely break them and their city'."

This made the priests so furious that the chief priest ordered Jeremiah beaten and put into the stocks.

Meanwhile the armies of Nebuchadnezzar, king of Babylon, were marching closer.

Now God told Jeremiah to write down all the prophecies he had delivered up to that time. So Jeremiah called his scribe Baruch and began dictating. When the scroll was finished, since Jeremiah was no longer allowed to speak in the temple, he sent Baruch to read it to the people.

When Baruch finished reading the scroll, a

prince asked him to read it to the assembly of the princes. When they had heard the whole thing, they said, "We must report all these words to the king. Give us the scroll. Since he will be angry, Baruch, you and Jeremiah must hide—let no one know where you are."

Then the princes delivered the scroll to the king, who was sitting in his winter house before a roaring fireplace. The princes gathered around him and a servant began reading. When he came to the words, "The king of Babylon will come and destroy this land, taking away man and beast," the king rose up in anger, took out a knife, cut off that part of the scroll, and threw it into the fire.

From then on, each time three or four columns were read, the king would cut them off and throw them into the flames. Three of the princes urged him not to destroy the scroll, but he ignored them.

When the entire scroll had been consumed by the blaze, the king ordered that Jeremiah and Baruch be seized, but they were already far away.

Then the word of the Lord came to Jeremiah: "Take another scroll and write on it everything that was on the first, plus this, that I will surely do all that I have said against Jerusalem."

Then God told Jeremiah to make a yoke for his neck as a sign to nearby nations that the Lord would give them all into the hand of Nebuchad-nezzar, that they must all wear the yoke of service to the king of Babylon. And to his own nation

Jeremiah was to say, "The Babylonian forces will be here soon. When they arrive, our army must give in, for God has declared that we must be under their power for a time. As for the towns-people, our only hope now is to flee the city."

When the leaders heard this, they hurried to the king and said, "If the people listen to Jeremiah and leave, the soldiers guarding the city will think all is lost and give up."

The king thought about this, then said, "Jeremiah has been nothing but trouble to us. If he keeps on, the city will certainly be lost. Yet one cannot help admiring his courage. Well, do with him what you must."

So they took Jeremiah out to an old cistern that had not been used for many years. It had only a little water and a layer of silt in the bottom. They threw Jeremiah in, and he sank several feet into the mire. Then they put the lid back on and left him there to die.

Several days later a servant in the king's house overheard two of the men talking about what they'd done. He hurried out to the cistern and lifted the lid. Far below he could see Jeremiah, half buried in mud, reduced almost to skin and bones. With the help of friends, he dropped down a padded rope for the emaciated prophet to tie around his bony frame, and they pulled him out.

Finally the day came when the Babylonian army reached the gates of Jerusalem and came thundering in. Up and down the streets they went, stealing whatever they wanted, setting fires, killing many people. When the battle was over, they carried away as captives the king, the princes, and all the skilled workers and healthy young people, leaving behind the old, the crippled, and others who would be of no use to them. Jeremiah, given the option, chose to stay with those left behind.

Life was hard for the exiles. Assigned places to live along the old, unused canals of the city of Babylon, they had to cope with disease-bearing mosquitoes and hot, humid days. Temperatures sometimes soared to 110 degrees. They were completely cut off from their homeland and from their relatives and friends. When they began to feel sorry for themselves, God had Jeremiah write them:

> Thus says the Lord to all the exiles sent from Jerusalem: Do not despair; build homes, plant gardens, enjoy your families, and seek the wellbeing of the city in which you find yourselves, for in its wellbeing you will find your own.

But they also felt cut off from their God. They were used to going up to the temple in Jerusalem to be in God's presence, sometimes taking their lyres with them to add joyous music to their worship. Now they knew no way of coming into God's presence. The Babylonians would say to them, "Play on your lyres and sing us some of your songs," but they could not sing the Lord's song in a foreign land. By the waters of Babylon they sat down and wept.

So Jeremiah wrote to them that they didn't have to be in a temple to pray, that God is with his people wherever they are—even with captives in a strange land—and that in time, when they learned to be God's people again, he would bring them once more to their homeland.

"God will make a new covenant with you," he told them, "but not like the old covenant which you broke. This time God will write his law, not on tablets of stone, but on your hearts."

Then Jeremiah gave them God's promise of the coming Savior: From the family tree of David would come a mighty branch, one who would rule with wisdom and justice and righteousness.

Toward the end of Jeremiah's life, some of the people left in Judah rose up in revolt against the Babylonians. They met strong opposition, and they planned to flee to Egypt. Jeremiah told them that if they stayed all would be well with them, but if they went they would surely die.

Ignoring his warning, they insisted they were going and that he must come with them. When he refused, they tied him up and took him to Egypt as their prisoner. They never had been willing to follow the messages Jeremiah brought from God, but they did want to know what the messages were.

Tradition has it that Jeremiah died a martyr, probably in the land of Egypt. For more than 40

years, with no thought of his own safety, he faith-
fully delivered God's messages to his people. He
heard God's call as a young man and spent his
life serving him, living out the words, "Let not
the wise man glory in his wisdom or his might
or his riches, but let him glory in this, that he
understands and knows me."

The Book of Jeremiah

Theme: God wants his covenant people to return
to him.

I. Jeremiah's early ministry (1–25).

    A. His visions and warnings to his people, who
have turned from God (1-10).

    B. Events in his life (11–12).

    C. His parables and teachings (13–25).

II. Jeremiah's later ministry (26–52).

    A. His conflicts with the religious leaders over
what God wants the people to do (26–29).

    B. Comfort, warnings, examples, and prom-
ises (30–35).

    C. Concluding events (36–52).
        1. Jeremiah's scroll read (36).
        2. Siege and fall of Jerusalem (37–41).
        3. Jeremiah's flight to Egypt (42–52).

Ezekiel

The Bones
That Rattled into Life

As Ezekiel watched, a great cloud rolled out of the north, in its center a throne over which hovered cherubim. A form like a person appeared on the throne and increased in brightness until, in a blaze of light, the glory of the Lord broke forth. Ezekiel fell to his face on the ground.

Then a voice said, "Stand up and I will speak with you." When Ezekiel was standing, the voice said, "I am sending you to the people of Israel, to his nation that has rebelled against me and committed every sort of violence, and you shall say to them, 'Thus says the Lord.' And whether they listen or refuse to listen (for they are a rebellious people), they will know there has been a prophet among them."

Then a scroll inscribed with words of lamentation and mourning and woe was held out to Ezekiel and he was told to eat it. He tasted it and found it sweet as honey. When he had swallowed the last word, the voice spoke more directly. "I must tell you that though I send you to speak to my people, they will not listen. But do not be afraid—I have given you the strength to stand up against them."

As Ezekiel stood, awestruck, the cloud began moving back up into the heavens with the sound as of a great earthquake. When the last traces of the cloud had disappeared at a far point in the sky, Ezekiel went back to be among his people, Israel. He sat for seven days among them, overwhelmed.

At the end of the seven days, the word of the Lord came to him again. "I have made you a watchman for the people of Israel. Whenever you hear a word from my mouth, you must warn them, or you will be responsible for their wrongdoing. Meanwhile, I shall make you dumb; only when I give you a word to say to them will your tongue be loosened."

Then Ezekiel was told to perform a series of symbolic acts to warn his people. First he was to take clay and make a brick, drawing on it a picture of Jerusalem, then set up mounds and walls against it as though it were besieged by enemies. He was then to lie down, first on his left side on behalf of the Northern Kingdom for 390 days (perhaps only for a brief length of time each day), then on his right side for the Southern Kingdom for 40 more days, each day to symbolize a year of punishment that was coming for Israel.

Then he was to shave his head and beard as though he were a captive (instead of a priest, which was his calling), dividing the hair into thirds, burning the first, striking the second with a sword, and scattering the third to the wind, symbolizing what was to happen to the people as a result of their wickedness. Israel would be a horror and a warning to all the surrounding nations. If God couldn't reveal himself to the other nations through an obedient Israel, he would reveal himself by judging a rebellious Israel.

What had Israel been doing to deserve all this? The people had committed every sort of crime, dealing violently and unjustly with each other, and they had fallen into the pagan practices of neighboring nations, worshiping that which was not worthy of their worship.

Then in a vision Ezekiel saw a man clothed in linen, symbolizing holiness, going through the city, placing a mark on the forehead of each person who lamented the wickedness of the city. He was followed by executioners who slew all who did not have the mark. Then the man clothed in linen took burning coals from the throne and scattered them over the city to cleanse it from its guilt. Ezekiel tried to warn the people about these things, but they would not listen.

So God had Ezekiel try other methods. He dressed like an exile, carrying an exile's baggage and eating an exile's rations, going out of his house through a hole he had dug in the wall. He cautioned the prophets of Israel not to give the people false assurance, not to tell them that all would be well. He warned Israel that God would send the king of Babylon to carry them away as captives if they continued in their faithless way. But they paid no attention.

God knew what the people were saying. They were saying, "It's our fathers who did wrong, not us. Surely God wouldn't bring calamity upon us for wrong our fathers did."

But God told Ezekiel to tell them, "You yourselves have done wrong, and you yourselves will be brought low for it. Each of you is responsible for what you do; each of you will have to answer fully for yourself before me." But the people still paid no attention.

"Can't you remember," God asked, "how I set you free from slavery in the land of Egypt and led you through the sea and the wilderness, making a covenant with you, and finally brought you into the promised land? Yet even as I was bringing you to the promised land, you began to rebel. You were like an abandoned child that I picked up and cared for, yet you turned aside from me to do wickedness." These words fell on uncaring ears.

In all these efforts to restore his people, God did not spare his prophet Ezekiel. One day he told Ezekiel that he was going to take the delight of his eyes away from him at a single stroke, and that he must not mourn. The next day as Ezekiel was still pondering what this might mean, his wife died. When, following God's instructions, he did not mourn, the people became very curious and asked him about it. He told them that in the same manner God would suddenly take away the delight of their eyes, their temple and the city of Jerusalem, and that when that day came they would be too deep in grief to mourn, that then they would know that the Lord is God.

God was concerned not only that his people return to him but that neighboring nations also learn to know him. Therefore he gave Ezekiel messages for all the nations nearby.

Finally the day came when God's judgment could be avoided no longer. The Babylonians swept down upon Jerusalem, destroying the temple and carrying many of the people to Babylon as captives. As exiles, the people groaned in their misery, mourning for their homeland and longing for freedom. "How can we go on living?" they asked. "Everything that was important to us is lost to us—our city, our homes, our temple—and here we are, strangers in a strange land."

Many began to give up in despair. Cut off from

their temple, they felt that they could no longer make contact with God. But God sent Ezekiel to say to them: "The presence of God is not restricted to a single place; God's presence can be experienced by believers no matter where they live."

Then God gave Ezekiel a vision of what could be, showing that out of destruction could come new hope. He took Ezekiel out to a valley that was strewn with bones. Ezekiel walked among bones that lay scattered in all directions; he could see that they were very dry.

Then God asked, "Can these bones live?" To Ezekiel they looked as dry and unpromising as Israel's hopes for the future—he could only answer that only God alone could know. Then God said, "Say to these bones, 'Hear the word of the Lord, for I will cause breath to enter you, and you will live. I will cause sinews and flesh and skin to come upon you, and you will live and know that I am the Lord.'"

So Ezekiel spoke these words to the bones. Immediately there was a great rattling, and the bones began reassembling themselves to make human bodies, gradually covering with sinews and flesh and skin. But there was no breath in them. Then the Lord spoke the word and they breathed and stood upon their feet, a very large number of people.

And God said, "These are the people of Israel. All hope is not lost for them. As I restored these bones, so will I restore you, my people, and at length I will bring you home again to the land of Israel. And I will give you a new heart and a new spirit, and you will live; and you will know that I am the Lord. You will be my people, and I will be your God."

Then God gave Ezekiel a vision of how the temple in Jerusalem should be rebuilt. As a priest, Ezekiel was especially concerned that the people have a fitting place for worship. But God wanted them to do more than worship; he wanted them to put away violence and oppression and begin practicing justice and righteousness. Then the temple, representing God's presence among them, could be a center from which could flow a river like the river of the Garden of Eden, like the river in the book of Revelation, a river of life bringing healing and life to all the nations, with each redeemed and renewed person doing God's will on earth.

The Book of Ezekiel

Theme: You will be my people so that all nations will know that I am the Lord.

I. God's judgment on Judah and Jerusalem (1–24).
   A. Ezekiel is called and commissioned (1–3).
   B. Jerusalem will go into exile because it has turned from God's way (4–24).

II. God will also judge foreign nations (25–32).
   A. Ammon, Moab, Edom, and Philistia (25).
   B. Tyre and Sidon (26–28).
   C. Egypt (29–32).

III. God will restore Israel (33–39).
   A. Each person has responsibility for himself and for all (33–35).
   B. God will restore his people in their land, that all nations may know he is Lord (36–39).

IV. The restored community will witness to the living God (40–48).
   A. How the new temple should be built (40–43).
   B. How priests and people are to conduct life inside and outside the temple (44–46).

Daniel

The Man
Who Lodged with Lions

When King Nebuchadnezzar besieged Jerusalem
and carried many of its most promising people as
captives back to Babylon, among the group was
a young man named Daniel. Nebuchadnezzar
was determined to have Daniel and his friends
instructed in the Babylonian language and cus-
toms so they could serve in the palace, but Daniel
was determined to do nothing that would upset
his relationship with God.

This created some problems, such as in the
matter of eating. When Daniel resolved that he
would not pollute his body with the king's rich
food, the eunuch watching over Daniel's health
became greatly alarmed. "You must eat the things
the king has assigned for you," he protested. "If

you stop looking healthy, the king will demand my head."

But Daniel had an idea. "Make a test for 10 days," he urged. "Let us have only the vegetables and water we're used to, and at the end of that time see how we look." The eunuch was hesitant, but Daniel persisted.

When the 10 days were up, the eunuch was relieved to see that Daniel and his friends not only looked healthy—they looked much more vigorous than the young men who ate rich delicacies. Not only that, but God had given them understanding so that when the king spoke to them, he found them superior in wisdom and understanding to all the wise men of his kingdom.

But Daniel's troubles were not over. The king had a dream one night, and in the morning he called wise men and seers to him, demanding they not only interpret the dream but also tell him what the dream was. The wise men and seers paled at this. "Tell us the dream," they said, "and we will give you its interpretation."

But the king held his ground. "If you do not make known to me both the dream and its interpretation, I will have you torn limb from limb."

His wise men pleaded with him, "There's not a person alive who can tell what your dream was, and no king on earth has ever demanded such a thing. Only the gods could possibly know the answer and their dwelling is not with people."

This made the king furious, and he commanded

that all his wise men, including Daniel and his friends, be put to death. When Daniel heard this, he gathered his friends to pray for God's help. Then he saw in a vision of the night both the dream and its interpretation. He hurried to the king and said, "The God of heaven has revealed to me your dream. You saw a large statue with a head of gold, upper body and arms of silver, lower body and thighs of bronze, legs of iron, and feet partly of iron and partly of clay. Then a great stone struck the image and shattered it, and the stone became a great mountain.

"And this is its interpretation: You are the head of gold. After you shall rise other kingdoms, each weaker than the one before, until God sets up a kingdom that shatters and supersedes all the others, a kingdom that shall never be destroyed."

Then the king said, "Truly, your God is God of gods," and he made Daniel chief over all the wise men of the country. His friends Shadrach, Meshach, and Abednego were also given positions of authority.

But still Daniel and his friends' problems were not over. The king set up a huge statue of gold and commanded that when the people heard the sound of various musical instruments, everyone must worship the statue, warning that those who did not would be thrown into the fiery furnace. Certain men, jealous of the high position Shadrach, Meshach, and Abednego had attained, noticed one day that they were not worshiping the image. Gleefully they hurried to tell the king. Nebuchadnezzar was angered by the news and called Shadrach, Meshach, and Abednego before him.

"Is it true," he asked, "that you will not worship the golden image? If you will, well and good. If not, I'll have to have you thrown into the fiery furnace."

Shadrach, Meshach, and Abednego answered, "God is able to deliver us, even from the fiery furnace. But even if he chooses not to, we will not worship the golden image."

This made the king even more angry. He ordered the furnace heated up seven times as hot and the three thrown into it. The furnace was so hot that the men who bound up Shadrach, Meshach, and Abednego and threw them in were burned to death.

Then, as the king watched, he noticed with alarm that something strange was going on.

"Didn't I have three men thrown in?" he asked one of his counselors. He was told that this was so. "But I see four men," he exclaimed, "walking around in the fire unhurt! And the appearance of the fourth is like a son of the gods."

Then Nebuchadnezzar went near the door of the furnace and commanded, "Shadrach, Meshach, and Abednego, servants of the Most High God, come forth!" They came out, and not one of them was hurt. Their hair was not singed nor their clothing burned.

Then the king said, "Blessed be the God of Shadrach, Meshach, and Abednego, who has sent his angel and delivered his servants, who trusted in him" (3:28). And he issued a decree that any people, nation, or language that spoke anything against the God of Shadrach, Meshach, and Abednego should be torn limb from limb.

Then the king had another dream, and again his wise men were no help—Daniel was the only one able to tell him what it meant. Daniel explained that the king was the great tree that would be cut down with only a stump remaining, that his throne and his mind would be taken from him and he would be driven away from people to live in the fields and eat grass like an animal, until he understood "that the Most High rules the kingdom of men, and gives it to whom he will."

In a few months this came true, and for a long time Nebuchadnezzar wandered about mindlessly in the wilderness. Then one day he lifted his eyes to heaven. His reason returned and he blessed the Most High and was able to go back to rule his kingdom.

After Nebuchadnezzar died, his son Belshazzar came to power in Babylon and made a great feast. Arrogantly he ordered the vessels of gold and silver that had been stolen from the temple in Jerusalem brought forth so he and his guests could drink wine from them.

Suddenly handwriting began appearing on the wall: MENE, MENE, TEKEL, PARSIN. Belshazzar was seized with fear and called for his wise men. All of them tried to decipher the words but could not. Then Daniel was called in.

"You have lived as arrogantly as your father," Daniel told him, "defying the Lord by misusing the vessels from his altar. You have been weighed in the balances and found wanting, and therefore your kingdom will be divided and given to others."

Though this news was not welcome, Belshazzar gave Daniel an even higher position in the kingdom for relaying it to him. And that very night Belshazzar was slain and Darius the Mede became king in his place.

Now the other officials of the kingdom, jealous of Daniel's great power, tried to find some way to bring him down. Finally, knowing Daniel's devout ways, they got the king to pass an ordinance that whoever prayed to anyone but the king would be thrown to the lions.

Daniel, though he knew about the ordinance, continued to get down on his knees and pray to God three times a day. When the men caught him doing so, they reported it to the king. The king was greatly distressed and tried to find a way to keep from having to carry out the ordinance, but the law was binding. Finally he ordered Daniel thrown into the lions' den.

That night the king was sleepless, worrying about Daniel. As soon as it was morning, he hurried to the den and called out, "Daniel, servant of the living God, has your God been able to save you?"

"O king, live forever," came the reply. "My God shut the lions' mouths, and they have not hurt me."

Then the king ordered Daniel taken out and those who had accused him thrown in with their families. The lions grabbed them and they perished before they hit the bottom of the den. And the king sent out a decree that all nations should worship the living God.

Then Daniel himself had a dream in which he saw four beasts, each representing a kingdom, coming up out of the sea. He saw the Ancient of Days sitting in judgment, giving final dominion to one like a son of man and the kingdom to the saints of the Most High.

Daniel had another vision of a ram with two horns and a he-goat, representing Media, Persia, and Greece and their struggle for power. And yet another vision concerned further struggles for dominance by eastern Mediterranean countries.

Finally Daniel was told that at the end time the wicked will arise from the dust of the earth to shame, but those whose names are written in the book will arise to everlasting life. "But shut up the words," he was told, "and seal the book until the time of the end, when those who are wise will shine like the brightness of the firmament."

The Book of Daniel

Theme: God is at work throughout history, building his kingdom.

I. Six stories about Daniel and his friends (1–6).

    A. Daniel and his friends join Nebuchadnezzar's court (1).

    B. Daniel interprets Nebuchadnezzar's dream of a great statue (2).

    C. Shadrach, Meshach, and Abednego are thrown into the fiery furnace (3).

    D. Daniel interprets Nebuchadnezzar's dream about the great tree (4).

    E. Daniel interprets the handwriting on the wall at Belshazzar's feast (5).

    F. Daniel is thrown into the lions' den (6).

II. Daniel's four visions (7–12).

    A. The four beasts (7).

    B. The ram and the he-goat (8).

    C. The 70 weeks (9).

    D. The last days (10–12).

Hosea's Weird Marriage

Hosea, the bachelor prophet, lived a peaceful existence, each day much like the one before and the one after, nothing spectacular ever happening. Then one day God suddenly threw a bombshell into his life. Out of the blue, God pitched him a weird assignment: *Go marry a prostitute.*

Hosea couldn't believe he was hearing right!

In the first place, he wasn't sure he wanted to get married at all. But to be joined in marriage —he, a servant of God—with a prostitute? He couldn't imagine such a thing! What was God trying to do?

God explained he had to do something drastic to show his people, the children of Israel, that they were playing the harlot to him. Lately they had completely turned their backs on him, practicing all sorts of wickedness and worshiping Baal. No longer did they even come into his holy temple; instead they flocked to tree-topped hills and bowed down to idols.

The people of Hosea's day weren't much different from us today. Things were so good, they had so much more than they needed, that they thought they could ignore God and their covenant with him. During the hard years, when they'd been traveling from Egypt to their promised land, they had depended on God directly each day for all their needs—food, water, even directions for the day's travel. But when they reached their rich land, it became easy to think of themselves as self-sufficient. They didn't realize they still needed God. They hadn't caught on to the truth that we need more than bread to live.

God longed for the day when they would return to him.

So Hosea went and married Gomer, a prostitute, and she bore a son. Hosea named him Jezreel as God had instructed, for God planned to punish Israel by letting it be defeated in the valley called Jezreel.

When Gomer presented Hosea with a daughter, the Lord told him to name her Not Pitied, to show that God had lost his compassion for Israel. When she had another son God ordered

Hosea to call him Not My People, explaining, "Israel is not mine and I am not Israel's God."

God could not let the chosen people go on in sin. If they could see their depravity and unfaithfulness acted out in Hosea's marriage, perhaps they would see how far they had fallen and return to God. Hosea represented God, the faithful one. Gomer represented the unfaithful people of Israel who went lusting after other husbands (gods). Their children were the natural fruit of such a relationship—suffering, sorrow, and separation from God.

God let the lesson sink in. He waited for his people to realize the symbolic meaning of Hosea's marriage. As a catalyst to speed their awakening, God made life hard for them; he caused the grain in the fields to develop with no heads, and the people cried out for food. He turned allied nations against the Israelites and let their enemies attack and kill many of them. When children were born, God let them sicken and die. If prosperous times had wooed the people away from him, maybe difficult times would lead them back.

God sat and watched, waiting for the day when the people who had turned from him would be called "sons of the living God," when they would turn from their evil ways to walk again in his path. He promised that when they returned to him, he would make their land flourish—their fields would bear much grain, their children would grow and be strong. They would once more be his favored people, and he would be their revered God.

Sometimes God has spoken to his people with a still, small voice, as he did with Elijah; sometimes from a burning bush, as to Moses; sometimes with a dramatic acting out of the utter unfaithfulness of his people, as in Hosea's offbeat marriage.

A strange assignment—to marry a prostitute. God could hardly have chosen a more dramatic method to open the eyes of his people.

The Book of Hosea

Theme: God loves his people, though they are faithless, and calls them back.

I. Hosea's strange marriage (1–3).

    A. Hosea marries a prostitute who bears three children who are not his (1:1-9).

    B. Israel has been adulterous, but can be restored (1:10—2:1).

    C. God calls his people back (2:2-23).

    D. As Hosea buys back his adulterous wife, so will God buy back his people (3).

II. Israel's unfaithfulness to God (4–13).

    A. The people and their priests are corrupt (4:1—7:7).

    B. Israel has sown the wind and will reap the whirlwind (7:8—10:15).

    C. God continues to love his people (11:1-11).

    D. If Israel will acknowledge him, God will restore her to abundant life (11:12—13:16).

III. God calls Israel to return to him (14).

    A. The Lord says, Return to me (14:1-3).

    B. He promises to restore them (14:4-9).

The Role
of Joel

"Listen! What's that noise? And what's happened
to the sun all of a sudden? It's like night! Grasshoppers? Grasshoppers! Get them out of here!
They're down my back! They're crawling up my
legs! Oof—I think there's one in my ear!"

A deplorable situation.

But this was not the worst of it. In a short
while the grasshopperlike locusts devoured everything green (hurrah, no more broccoli!), and
were proceeding to other colors.

Close at their heels came the scorching sun,
searing whatever had escaped the hoppers' near-
sighted scrutiny.

The land lay like Mother Hubbard's cupboard
—empty.

"When do we eat?" was replaced by "*What* do we eat?"

The answer was the same everywhere. "Nothing."

At a time like this, if at no other time, people may turn to God, which gives us some idea of why God portions out such adversity.

The land of Israel was in a mess because the people had forgotten God and his teachings. To bring them back to himself, God planned something drastic—the gnawing of locusts, the pangs of hunger, the shriveling drouth. The people were ready to listen as their prophet, Joel, brought them words from God:

"This plague—has such a monstrous thing happened in your days, or even in the days of your fathers? The destruction has been utter. What the cutting locust left, the swarming locust has eaten. What the swarming locust left, the hopping locust has eaten. and what the hopping locust left, the destroying locust has eaten. Your fields are laid waste; the ground mourns; the harvest has perished."

Then Joel told the clergy what to do: "Dress yourselves in sackcloth and plead with God. Declare a fast. Gather the elders and all the inhabitants of the land to the house of the Lord your God, and cry unto him. He is merciful. Perhaps if you truly repent and return unto him, he will put an end to this desolation."

The priests put on sackcloth and besought

God: "Spare your people, O Lord. Don't let the heathen nations be able to laugh and say, 'Where is this God they say they believe in? Can't he help them?' "

When the Lord saw they were truly repentant, he had pity on them and told Joel to tell the people, "Behold, I am sending to you grain, wine, and oil. You shall eat in plenty and be satisfied, and praise the name of the Lord your God, who has dealt wondrously with you. And you shall know that I, the Lord, am your God, and there is none else" (from 2:19, 26-27).

God used this occasion—the infestation of grasshoppers—not only to bring the people back to a living relationship with himself, but also to prepare them for judgment day:

"I will give portents in the heavens and on the earth, blood and fire and columns of smoke. The sun shall be turned to darkness, and the moon to blood, before the great and terrible day of the Lord comes. And it shall come to pass that all who call upon the name of the Lord shall be delivered" (2:30-32).

"For behold, in those days I will gather . . . all the nations and bring them down to the valley of Jehoshaphat, and I will enter into judgment with them there" (3:1-2).

But God promised that before that day he would send his Holy Spirit:

"And it shall come to pass afterward, that I will pour out my spirit on all flesh; your sons and your daughters shall prophesy, your old men shall dream dreams, and your young men shall see visions" (3:28).

And so God, through Joel, had brought his people once more back to himself.

As for the locusts, God shunted them off into the desert of Arabia, from which, in due time, a stench wafted clear back to Israel. But the stench was perfume to the delivered Israelites. The grasshopper scourge was over. The people were once more ready to serve God with their whole hearts.

The Book of Joel

Theme: God will pour out his Spirit on all believers.

I. A plague of locusts has settled on the land (1:1—2:27).

    A. The people and the earth mourn (1).

    B. The locust attack is a warning of the coming Day of the Lord (2:1-11).

    C. Joel calls his people to repent so God can restore them (2:12-27).

II. God will bless his people (2:28—3:21).

    A. He will pour out his Holy Spirit on them (2:28-29).

    B. In the day of the Lord, all people will be judged (2:30—3:16a).

    C. God is a refuge to his people (3:16b-21).

Why Amos
Is Famous

It was an unusual assignment: *Hightail it to the neighboring country and warn the people they're bringing down disaster upon themselves.*

But Amos packed and went.

Upon reaching Bethel, he climbed up on whatever was used for a soapbox in those days and began:

"You have become rich and have forgotten many things. Look at you! You hate to see the Sabbath come because you're so greedy to earn more money that you can't even take time out to go to worship! You cheat your customers by loading the bottoms of the grain sacks with stones! You water down the milk! You give the scales a sly assist with your thumb when you weigh purchases! You sell the poor into slavery the moment they can't pay their bills! You care not one iota for those who suffer! You sell the penniless for a pair of shoes!

"You are well-to-do and proud of it, but in your soul is famine.

"You began as God's chosen ones; now all that is forgotten. You waste your lives in chasing pleasure, in piling up even more wealth, in stomping on the poor—all the time drifting further from the God who made you.

"You are no better than cattle!

"Mark my words: there is no end to all this but decay and death!"

At this point at least one of the listeners had heard enough. Ready to blow a fuse, Amaziah, the local priest, dispatched a messenger. "Go tell the king that Amos is conspiring against him, predicting the king will be killed by a sword, that Israel will be conquered, and that all the people will be led away as slaves!"

Without waiting to see the courier off, Amaziah rammed his way through the crowd. How dare this young upstart Amos come into his parish and carry on so!

He stormed up to the front and grabbed Amos by the shoulder of his shepherd's garb. "All right," he growled, "get moving! We don't need your half-baked ideas around here. Go back to where you came from and prophesy there. Maybe they have a little more stomach for your words than we do!"

Amos did not budge. He just went on giving his message: "I was neither a prophet nor the son of a prophet, but a sheepherder and keeper of a fig orchard, until the day God called me and said, 'Go, prophesy to my people Israel.' God has sent me here to tell you these things, and I'm not through yet. Therefore, hear the words of the Lord!"

Turning again to his audience, Amos put the finishing touches on his sermon.

"You have forgotten God. Behold, he will send a famine upon your land; not a famine of bread, but a famine of hearing the words of the Lord. You shall wander from sea to sea and from north to south to seek the word of the Lord, and you shall not find it.

"Behold, the eyes of the Lord God are upon this sinful kingdom, and he will destroy it off the face of the earth, saving only the house of Jacob."

Having completed his message, Amos climbed down off his soapbox and went back to Tekoa to tend his flocks, thus ending one of the shortest preaching campaigns on record.

How effective was his speech?

Seemingly no one paid too much attention to what he said. Israel, carrying on in its same blind way, was overcome by an invader and led away into captivity—just as Amos had foretold. But during their days in slavery the people remembered Amos' words, repented, and were restored to God and ultimately to their homeland.

And Amos, the quiet, rural servant of God, lived out his days peacefully among his sheep and sycamore trees, writing the book that we carry around in our Bibles today. Amos started a fire in the hearts of God's people that was never to go out.

The Book of Amos

Theme: Human life finds its meaning in God.

I. God will judge all peoples (1–2).

    A. Neighboring peoples (1:1–2:3).

    B. Israel's neighbor Judah (2:4-5).

    C. Israel itself (2:6-16).

II. God will punish Israel for its sinfulness (3–6).

    A. God's people have a responsibility (3).

    B. They have not lived as God's people (4).

    C. Therefore God will bring them down in order to bring them back (5–6).

III. God will judge his people and restore them (7–9).

    A. God will send locusts and fire (7:1—8:3).

    B. God will send a famine of hearing the words of the Lord (8:4-14).

    C. God's people will go into captivity (9:1-7).

    D. God will restore a remnant of his people (9:8-15).

Obadiah

An
Unmighty
Fortress

Bang! Grind! Clash! High in the jagged mountains of Edom, a determined band of men, up before dawn, hurriedly lashed on their swords and shields. A last look at their city, strategically set among the rugged cliffs, then on to battle.

After an unusually bloody conflict, the city of Jerusalem was theirs, and they dashed from house to house, seizing whatever caught the eye.

Then, towering over their pleading victims, they burst into derisive laughter.

Laughter?

Had they forgotten that they and the Israelites were brothers and sisters? How could descendants of Esau deal so treacherously with descendants of his twin, Jacob?

Nor was this their first raid. On several other infamous occasions, the fighting men of Edom swept down out of their mountain fortress south of the Dead Sea in what is today the kingdom of Jordan and plundered the Israelites.

Was there to be no end to this family feud?

Certainly it was a sad historical fact that Esau had given over his birthright to Jacob for the ancient equivalent of stew, and that Jacob had later tricked his father Isaac into also giving him the family blessing. Old Isaac, blind as he was, could hardly be blamed—with goatskin tied securely in place, Jacob's neck and arms *felt* like Esau's hairy ones.

In those days a birthright was nothing to be sniffed at. It gave the firstborn the right not only to inherit a double share of his father's property; it also passed on to him the leadership of the family or clan.

In the case of Jacob and Esau, the birthright meant something additional, something of even greater value. It meant the privilege of being in the line of ancestors of Christ, for God had promised Abraham that through him and his son Isaac and Isaac's son, the very Son of God would some day descend.

All this apparently failed to impress Esau. If he had thought enough of his birthright, he would not have traded it off so carelessly to his brother.

And now Esau's descendants, the Edomites,

were drifting along in the same spiritually care-less way. They no longer were even Jews. For all practical purposes, they had no religion. Business had become their god; the buying and selling of sheep and cattle had become their sole form of worship; and perhaps the only prayer that fell from their lips was, "Hail, Money, successor to God."

The Edomites had a long history of malice toward Israel. Back when Moses was leading the children of Israel out of Egypt into the promised land, he asked permission from the Edomites to pass through their land, which would have cut the length of the journey considerably.

When the men of Edom came charging out to meet them in full battle armor, Moses got his answer, and the Israelites took the long way around.

God was not drowsing during all this. He gave his prophet Obadiah these words to deliver to Edom: "You who live in the clefts of the rock, you who say 'No one will ever be able to bring us down from our impenetrable city'—to you I say, 'I will bring you down.' Behold, I will make you utterly despised among the nations."

God vowed to mete out to the Edomites the consequences of their cruelty. "Because of the violence you have done to your brother Jacob, you will live hereafter in shame, and in time I will sweep every one of you from off the face of the earth. There shall be no survivor of the house of Esau. As you have done, so shall it be done to you. Your deeds shall return upon your own head."

We do not know when, or where, or how Obadiah delivered this prophecy that is recorded in the shortest book of the Old Testament (one chapter, 21 verses), but history shows that the prophecy was fulfilled—and speedily. Just a few years later Edom was attacked and practically annihilated.

From the few survivors came the unsavory King Herods—no more saintly nor esteemed among the Israelites than the earlier Edomites.

In due time, not a single branch or twig remained upon the family tree of Edom. The men from the *un*mighty mountainside fortress were no more, just as Obadiah had prophesied.

Obadiah had just one more prophecy to make, one that stands today: "The Lord shall be King!"

The Book of Obadiah

Theme: The Lord is ruler over all.

I. God will judge Edom for its treacherousness (1-14).

    A. Edom will be brought down (1-4)

    B. And completely destroyed (5-9)

    C. Because its people did violence to their brothers (10-14).

II. The day of the Lord will come (15-21)

    A. Upon all people (15-16)

    B. But the Lord will save his people (17-21).

Jonah

The Fish
That Went Manning

There he was, cruising off to starboard of a ship
bound for Tarshish, Spain, the western boundary
of the then-known world. The slippery sea-scav-
enger was waiting for his promised dinner.

Dinner? Well, not quite. Jonah, the main item
on the menu, was a morsel intended to be tasted
and kept in storage rather than chewed and di-
gested.

Scene 1. The fish cocks his slippery ear. What
a commotion on board! A sudden storm had
blown up and was threatening to reduce the ship
to narrow gauge driftwood. Sailors and passen-
gers seemed to be vying for the distinction of
throwing the greatest quantity of goods overboard

to lighten the load. Voyagers ran this way and that, jostling each other in confusion.

All were frantic—except for one landlubber who lay peacefully snoring down in the hold. He awoke to a strong hand dealing him a rough shaking. It was the ship's master.

"How can you sleep at a time like this? The ship is about to go down! Get up and call on your God to help us!"

Jonah rubbed his eyes. He made an effort to get up, but a quick lurch of the ship threw him back into his bunk.

Meanwhile, on the upper deck, the ship's hands were casting lots, a common practice in those days, to see who was responsible for this overgrown thundersquall. The lot fell on Jonah.

Poking his head up through the hatch, Jonah was met by an angry mob.

"Why?" one of the men demanded. "Why have you done this?"

Jonah knew only too well. "I was running away. God ordered me to go to Nineveh and warn the people that unless they turn from their wicked ways, his punishment will fall on them."

"Nineveh!" one of the deck hands snorted, pointing over the stern. "That's back there!"

"I know," Jonah replied, a little sadly.

Nineveh, a city of over half a million, was the capital of the heathen world. Jonah was a Jew. The idea of preaching repentance to a heathen nation was most repugnant. Jonah thought only the Jews should be God's people. And besides, Nineveh was the enemy of his nation, and he was not about to help his nation's enemy.

A piece of sail, torn by the fury of the winds, dealt the runaway prophet a wet slap across the face. The sea flung itself at the cringing craft like a raging beast.

"What are we going to do with this renegade?" one of the mates demanded anxiously. "We'll all drown!"

With a roar like a mighty waterfall, an enormous wave surged over the rail, sending several men sprawling.

"Take me," Jonah ordered, "and throw me overboard. There's no use all of you losing your lives."

But no man laid hands on him.

In a last effort, the men on the oars pulled until their muscles cried out, but they could not bring the vessel to shore.

There was nothing else to do. With a heave ho, they pitched Jonah out. And the storm lifted.

This is where the fish took over.

For three days and three nights Jonah rolled around inside the sea monster, begging God's mercy. God heard, and he ordered the fish to heave up its passenger on the shore. The fish's part of the drama was now ended; Jonah still had several more scenes to play.

Scene 2. God spoke to Jonah a second time: "Go to Nineveh."

This time Jonah went. For three or four days

he traveled throughout the city of Nineveh preaching: "In 40 days this great beehive of humanity will be destroyed—unless you turn from your wickedness to God."

The people listened and determined to change their ways. Proclaiming a fast, from the king on down to the least in the kingdom, they dressed themselves and all their household animals in sackcloth and ashes.

"Let us all cry mightily unto God," proclaimed the king, "and turn from our evil ways. Who can tell if God will turn and repent and spare us from his fierce anger."

God did see their repentant hearts and he spared them. The people had listened to Jonah's warning. Was Jonah happy? See Scene 3.

Scene 3. Jonah was so angry, he could have demolished Nineveh all by himself. He poured out his wrath to God: "You sent me to tell Nineveh it would be annihilated. Now you aren't even going to hurt one hair of it! The people of Nineveh are wicked and they should be punished! I can't stand it! If you aren't going to kill them, I wish you'd kill me!"

Peeved and pouting, Jonah stomped out of the city and sat down to wait for its complete destruction.

And lo, God made a gourd vine to spring up and cool Jonah in its shade. Jonah rejoiced.

But God also prepared a worm, and the next morning before the sun was scarcely peeking over the horizon, the worm gnawed through the vine, and the vine withered. A scorching east wind and the blistering sun brought Jonah again to the point of desperation. "If only I could die!"

"Jonah!" the Lord called. "Are you angry about the gourd?" Jonah did not need to answer.

"You pity the gourd, you pity yourself," God went on, "and yet you have not one smidgen of pity for the city of Nineveh with its 120,000 small children? You would have me slay them, even after the people have changed their ways?"

God's words shamed Jonah. He had nothing left to say. Had his friend the fish still been around, he might have gladly climbed in. Only this time he wouldn't have needed a briny beast of such magnitude, because he felt very small.

The Book of Jonah

Theme: God's mercy and forgiveness extend to all people.

    I. Jonah is called to preach to Nineveh (1:1-16).

        A. He rebels and gets on a ship heading in the opposite direction (1:1-3).

        B. God intervenes with a storm; the sailors throw Jonah into the sea (1:4-16).

    II. Jonah's life is spared (1:17—2:10).

        A. A fish swallows him (1:17—2:9).

        B. He is delivered to dry land (2:10).

    III. Jonah preaches to Nineveh (3).

        A. The people listen and repent (3:1-9).

        B. God decides to spare them (3:10).

    IV. Jonah is angry that Nineveh is spared (4).

        A. Jonah complains to God for sparing them (4:1-3).

        B. God explains that his mercy is for all nations (4:4-11).

Bold Journey—
B. C. Style

Micah threw together the few necessary travel items—a goatskin to carry water, a slab of salt-cured fish, several pounds of dates, his rough woolen robe for a coat by day and blanket and mattress by night—and set off on foot for a dusty speaking tour of the country.

He didn't mind so much the long, hot walk, or making the speeches. Crowds seemed to form naturally whenever they heard he was going to bring a message from God. But once they got the drift of what he was saying . . .

Actually he wasn't presenting very popular stuff. Instead of a sweet syrupy message, Micah was tossing out remarks like: "You lie awake nights scheming how to get your neighbor's possessions—his fields and flocks and houses and barns—then you get up in the morning and do him out of them. You hate what is good and love what is evil. And you who are leaders are even worse; you treat the people as though they were animals for you to slaughter."

At this point in the address, a few of the listeners were bent over double—not with laughter, but for gathering suitable stones with which to pummel this offensive fellow. But Micah went right on:

"Watch out! God will come down and trample you underfoot, you who take widows' homes away from them to make yourselves richer, you who push orphans out to wander the streets because you are too selfish to share some of your great wealth with them!"

Suddenly a man in the back of the crowd raised a stone above his shoulder and took aim. Seeing him, Micah snatched up his few belongings from the ground and darted out of the crowd, out of town, and down the road toward the next one-night stand.

Too bad the people hadn't let him stay long enough to deliver the rest of the message—it had a bangup finish. (One of these days he was almost certain to find himself in a town without rocks.) He rehearsed the grand finale as he hiked along:

"Out of the little village of Bethlehem will come a great leader for Israel, one whose origin is from old, from ancient days." The promise that the Savior would come! Micah wondered when the great day of the Savior's appearance would be. Perhaps in *his* lifetime? Oh, to live to see him!

As he trudged along through the dust, he thought about the other prophecy God had given him to tell the people, that the day would come when the house of the Lord would be established, and people would flock toward it, people of all nations gathering to sing praises to God.

Overhead a silent-winged bird soared into the darkening sky. The moon was rising; the first stars were beginning to appear above the Judean hillside. Micah would have to hurry to reach the next little village before darkness engulfed the land.

He wondered what sort of audience he would find the next day, and if they would pick up stones. But the stones were of little concern compared to the message. Would they listen to his message, or would they harden their hearts? Oh, that they would listen and turn again to God!

The Book of Micah

Theme: He shall be great to the ends of the earth.

I. God will come (1:1-4).

   A. He will judge the people (1:1-2).

   B. His coming will melt the mountains (1:3-4).

II. God's people have forsaken his ways (1:5-16).

   A. The land shall be laid waste (1:5-9).

   B. The people will go into exile (1:10-16).

III. His people have become callous (2–3).

   A. They oppress the poor and unfortunate (2:1-11).

   B. Therefore, destruction and captivity will come upon them (2:12-13)

   C. And upon their leaders, who have helped bring this trouble on by their unrighteousness (3).

IV. But the kingdom of the Lord will be established (4–5).

   A. All nations shall take part in it (4).

   B. From Bethlehem shall come a ruler (5:1-6).

C. Israel will be a remnant among the nations (5:7-15).

V. God will restore his people (6–7).

    A. God's people have forgotten his saving acts of old and what it means to walk humbly with him (6).

    B. When God has chastised his people, he will restore them (7).

Nahum

The Wild West
of the East

See that ghost town over there? That used to be
Nineveh, one of the mightiest cities of the ancient
East. Glittering, glamorous Nineveh—a metropo-
lis of evil.

So powerful was Nineveh that she held many
nations in slavery to pamper her whims. Little
mattered to the people of Nineveh but their com-
fort and pleasure. Wickedness of every sort was
taken for granted: lying, stealing, adultery, mur-
der.

Finally, when the stench of her vanity and lies,
her robberies and foulness became unbearable to
God, he vowed he would destroy the city utterly.
And he did.

God didn't actually lift a finger against the city

himself; he just let it be known to the Medes and the Babylonians, Nineveh's enemies, that the Ninevites were so weakened by loose living that they could scarcely pick up a sword in their own defense.

The Medes and the Babylonians needed no further invitation. They hurriedly assembled armies and swept down on the city. A fearful sight in their bright red tunics and shields, the marauders raced through the streets in their chariots, here setting homes afire, there cutting down people with swords and spears. On they charged through the city, waving lighted torches and slinging them when they saw a likely target.

The city was large, but so was the army. After they had massacred the populace and scooped up all the valuables, they committed their final act against the city: they opened the gates of the dam that protected Nineveh. With a mighty roar, the waters of the Tigris surged in. Buildings toppled beneath the onrush, and the silt and sand borne by the water filled the spaces in between. The destruction of Nineveh was complete.

When the waters receded, only an occasional stone or clump of bricks protruded from the rolling acres of sand to hint that there had once been a mighty city. So thoroughly was Nineveh wiped off the map that for centuries it was lost to the world. Only a few nomads and a handful of lions knew about it.

The lions, with just a little digging, made lairs

among the ruins. Birds lodged in the upper protrusions of the buildings. From far off, wayfarers across that stretch of trackless expanse heard the growling and snarling of the lions and the weird crying of the cormorants and bitterns, and they went out of their way to avoid the place.

As the years passed, Bible scholars began wondering where this city had been located. (The destruction of Nineveh took place about 600 years before Christ.) About the middle of the 19th century, archeologists found the site.

As they worked, the city began to take shape —a house here, a stable there. Like a ghost town, Nineveh emerged from the sands. She stands today as a monument to the time God called a halt to the city's wickedness.

There was a prophet connected with the climactic episode in Nineveh's life. His name was Nahum, and he apparently lived in Galilee, the area where Jesus was to spend his boyhood some 600 years later. (Capernaum, "village of Nahum," may have been named for him.)

Like Jonah, Nahum carried a message from God to Nineveh. But Jonah's message had been of grace; Nahum's foretold certain doom. For a century and a half since the time of Jonah, God had prolonged the day of mercy, but the time had come when he had to settle accounts with Nineveh.

God sent Nahum a vision of all the things that would happen. Nahum doesn't tell us whether he went and warned Nineveh or simply wrote down what was to happen for the record. Perhaps God thought Nineveh had had enough warnings. Jonah, after his spectacular journey to Nineveh by fish, had given the city plenty of warning, and that time the people had repented. But soon they returned to their evil ways, and Nineveh was finally destroyed, just as God told Nahum it would be.

Nineveh, Wild West of the East, was so totally wiped out that she had to be dug up to even become a ghost town. It's like the cowboys say in the westerns, "You're such an ornery, lowdown critter they'd have to dig you up to bury you!"

The Book of Nahum

Theme: God is merciful, but his judgment is sure.

   I. God will avenge cruelty and immorality—in this case, that of Nineveh (1:1-14).

  II. Blessed are those who carry God's message (1:15).

III. Nineveh will be no more (2–3).
     A. The city will be attacked (2:1-5).
     B. Its people will flee and its treasures will be plundered (2:6-10).
     C. Because Nineveh has dealt treacherously with other nations (2:11-13)
     D. The city will be destroyed (3:1-4).
     E. The empire will pass away (3:5-19).

Habakkuk:
Tower Sitter

It was nearly harvest time and the vines were heavy with tempting grapes. Habakkuk was up in the tower of his vineyard watching for thieves. Suddenly he stamped his feet and fumed. The more he thought about it, the angrier he got.

He was angry with God—angry because the wicked people of the land were oppressing others unmercifully, and God was letting them do it.

Habakkuk could no longer stand to watch those in power committing violence of every sort. They cheated the people in business transactions every chance they got, robbed them of what little they had, lied about them and got them into trouble, even murdered them if it furthered their own plans. It was getting so that people expected life to be nothing but suffering.

And the wicked, wealthy, powerful ones could do all this without fear of punishment—no longer were the laws of the land enforced. Law cases were scheduled, but never came to trial—or, if they did, the decision was sure to favor those in power.

And so the wicked went their merry way, scoffing at God, worshiping idols, not missing any opportunity to take advantage of the common people.

Habakkuk just couldn't stand it any longer.

He opened his mouth and cried out in a loud voice to God, "How long will you let this go on? Can't you see what the wicked are doing? Why don't you put an end to this violence?"

He was probably a little startled when he heard God answering, "Don't worry, Habakkuk. Before long I'm going to give the wicked what they deserve—and in such a way that you'll hardly believe it. You know the Chaldeans. . . ."

Habakkuk nodded. He knew the Chaldeans. In all the world there was not a people fiercer or more terrible than the Chaldeans. The Chaldean horsemen were swifter than leopards, more vicious than the wolves that prowled the hills at night. The very mention of the word *Chaldeans* was enough to strike terror into the heart of the bravest man.

"At my leading," God went on, "the Chaldean

horsemen will come down upon the country with one goal in mind: violence. Like famished eagles they will sweep across the countryside, devouring everything in their path."

A chill ran down Habakkuk's backbone. He was going to make sure he was out of the way when the Chaldeans came!

"Just a minute!" God put in. "Before you settle down in your tower, I want you to write down these things I have told you. Write them plainly on tablets and show them to all the people. The righteous will read and know that I am true to my word, and will run to escape the destruction. The righteous will trust in me—and live!"

What about the wicked, those with no faith in God's promises? "The wicked will not be interested in reading a message from me," God went on. "They will laugh at what I say I am going to do, and while they are still laughing, they will be destroyed."

"When will all this happen?" Habakkuk wanted to know.

"At the appointed time," God assured him. "Wait for it. It will come."

So Habakkuk prepared the tablets and set them up in the marketplace where all could read them.

Some townspeople read the proclamation, gathered up their belongings, and hurried out of town. The unbelievers remained, scoffing at those who fled.

Reaching the top of his tower, Habakkuk

looked out over the beautiful land that rolled gently to the south, with groves of olive trees dotting the landscape. To the north the hills rose more steeply, the horizon crowned with the hazy peaks of a distant mountain range.

Habakkuk marveled how, here in God's wondrous creation, people could live lives vile beyond description. If only they knew God!

Then one day, as Habakkuk looked out from his tower, the Chaldeans came racing across the countryside on their frenzied horses—a fearful sight. They broke into homes, grabbed everything of value, murdered the people, and burned the buildings after them. Racing from house to house, they slaughtered and stole and set fires. Never, even in his wildest imagination, had Habakkuk seen anything so ferocious.

The valley below him was a mass of flames and smoke. Habakkuk plugged his ears to shut out the wailing of the victims. He tried to keep from inhaling the smoke that curled up into his tower. As he watched, the fury of the Chaldeans seemed to be increasing. On and on they rode, devastating every part of the broad valley. Habakkuk knew no one could survive such an onslaught. He only hoped the attackers would pass by far below without noticing his tower.

Then gradually the smoke cleared away and the invaders were gone. The valley lay in burned-out ruin, a wasteland devoid of people. Habakkuk remembered how he had cried to God to do something about the wicked, and how God had said he would destroy them in such a way that Habakkuk would hardly believe it.

God had done it. He had wiped out the wicked and spared his own, once more encouraging his people to walk in his way, once more encouraging them to live by faith.

"The righteous will trust in me—and live!" Habakkuk repeated to himself, as he climbed down from his tower. "The righteous will trust in me—and live!"

The Book of Habakkuk

Theme: At the proper time, God will deal with those who do wrong. Meanwhile the justified shall live by faith.

I. Why does God allow injustice? (1:1—2:3)
   A. "Why, God?" (1:1-4).
   B. "Wait and I'll show you" (1:5-11).
   C. "When?" (1:12—2:1).
   D. "In my good time. Wait for it" (2:2-3).

II. The justified person lives by faith (2:4-20).
   A. The righteous shall live, but the unrighteous shall fall (2:4-5).
   B. Many woes shall befall the nation or person that plunders (2:6-20).

III. A psalm of praise (3).
   A. I know your works, O Lord (3:1-3).
   B. I know your mighty power (3:4-9).
   C. I know your desire that your people find life (3:10-13).
   D. Therefore I will wait and trust in you (3:14-19).

God
Cleans
House

Zephaniah shook his head to clear the cobwebs out of his brain.

Had he heard right? Had God *really* said to him that he was going to destroy everyone—everyone in all the land?

Zephaniah could hardly believe it. He knew his was a wicked and unruly generation; people seemed to have reached an all-time low in lowdownness. Surely no group anywhere had ever been more violent and depraved.

But destroy *everyone?* It didn't seem fair!

And why? Why would God destroy *everyone?* What about those who were faithful to him? Certainly he wouldn't destroy *them?*

But Zephaniah had heard right. God said, "I

104

will slay *all* the people—not only those who worship idols, and those who have never sought me, and those who have been mine and have turned their backs on me, but even those who worship me."

Zephaniah was astounded! He could see why God might want to get rid of the wicked, but why would he do away with his followers?

God explained: "Because those who worship me are only half-hearted about it. They say, 'The Lord will not do good, neither will he do evil.' They go through the routine of worship without really believing that I am what I am. They're so lukewarm that they're not worth keeping alive."

"But—but—" Zephaniah pleaded, not wanting to see everyone perish, "if I went and told the people what you plan to do, perhaps they would come to their senses!"

"You can try. It may be that some will return to me and I will be able to spare them."

That was all Zephaniah wanted to know. Without waiting for further instructions, he hurried out to warn the people. In little towns and big, he gathered the people together and told them about the coming doom.

"We have turned away from God, and he is going to utterly destroy us all!" he warned. "He will leave no one alive! Our cities will become ruins on the desert. Not one of us will escape unless we return to God!"

"He's a raving madman!" someone in the audience shouted.

"He's been cutting wheat in the hot sun too long!" someone else yelled. "It's scrambled his brain!"

The crowd laughed and jeered.

"A madman! A madman!" they chanted. "Get moving, madman. We don't want you around here!"

But a few listened. A few recognized the truth in his words, and a few, in their hearts, turned again to God.

God looked down and saw them, and spoke again to Zephaniah: "I will save this remnant of the people. When I come to destroy the land, I will spare the lives of these few. From now on, they will be my people. I will rejoice over them and be their shepherd."

Zephaniah rejoiced too. There was sorrow in his heart for those who had shut their ears to his words and soon would be no more, but there was joy that once more, instead of having a lukewarm, deceitful, violent, idol-worshiping nation, God would have a people who would love him, who would be his own.

Zephaniah must have rejoiced too that, by walking around the country talking to people, he had been able to rescue a whole section of the population from destruction. Of course, *they* did the actual turning to God themselves, but Zephaniah had the satisfaction of knowing they would not have had the chance to be spared if he had not gone out to speak to them. Few prophets were given such a fearful and yet such a satisfying job.

God had cleaned house in the land of his chosen people. Once more they would truly be his followers.

The Book of Zephaniah

Theme: God will judge. His will shall prevail.

I. God will bring judgment upon his people (1).
   A. He will overthrow the wicked (1:1-6).
   B. He will overthrow those in high position who are fraudulent (1:7-9).
   C. He will judge those who say, "God is not concerned about this world" (1:10-13).
   D. The day of the Lord is coming (1:14-16)
   E. Bringing distress and a sudden end (1:17-18).

II. He will also judge the nations (2).
   A. The shameless will be driven away, the righteous spared (2:1-3).
   B. Therefore beware, Philistines, Moabites, Ammonites, Ethiopians (2:4-15).

III. The will of God will prevail (3).
   A. Those who are rebellious and defiled will be brought down (3:1-8).
   B. The nations will be converted, and a righteous remnant will be left in Israel (3:9-13).
   C. God's people will dwell in peace (3:14-20).

Are You Putting Your Money in a Bag Full of Holes?

Something strange was going on in the land of Judah. There wasn't a lot to eat because the crops had failed, but the funny part was that what food they had didn't satisfy anyone's hunger. Though people ate and ate, they still felt hungry.

And it wasn't just food that seemed bewitched. On chilly days, though people piled on more and more clothes, they couldn't get warm. Farmers planted more and more seed in hope of getting at least some sort of a crop, but almost nothing came up anyway. Money was nearly worthless, and none of the people had enough to buy the things they needed.

People had never seen anything like it. There was certainly something strange going on—something weird, something that couldn't be explained.

Then one day Haggai came to Jerusalem, climbed up on a box in the marketplace, and began speaking to the people:

"Are you eating more lately, but never getting full? Are you buying more and more clothes, yet never having enough to wear? And you who work for wages—does your money slip through your hands so fast that it seems like you're bringing home your pay in a bag full of holes? You never have enough of anything, and you can't imagine why?"

His audience was right with him, so Haggai loosened his desert-style headdress a notch and went on. "I'll give you a hint. Take a look at that building over there."

The people turned to look although they already knew what they'd see—the temple, or at least what *used to be* the temple. It had been reduced to a pile of rubble many years before, and no one had cared enough to build it up again. Once a magnificent building, it now lay in shambles, a confusion of stones littering the ground.

"If you still wonder why things aren't going right for you," Haggai added, "I'll give you a second hint. Think for a moment about what your own homes look like." He knew that most of them were proud of their beautiful homes.

"Is it right that you keep making your homes even more beautiful, and the temple lies in ruins?

You keep saying that some day you'll rebuild the house of God, but you never get around to it. How many years has it been since you and your children have had a place in which to worship? Because you have no temple, you have drifted far from God.

"God has sent blight to shrivel your crops, mildew to rot them, and hail to dash them to pieces, hoping you would turn to him for help. But you have not. He has sent drought—the rains ceased and the dew dried up—yet you have gone on ignoring him. He has sent sickness and death among you and your children, yet you would not call upon him."

Haggai looked over the audience and was amazed: the people were still listening!

"Now," he proceeded, "God says it is time to rebuild his house, time you had a place in which to come into his presence and learn of him. Therefore, God commands you to go up into the hills and bring wood to build his house."

The people took Haggai's message to heart. They began thinking about how far they had slipped from God—and so did Zerubbabel, the governor of Judah, and Joshua, the high priest, who immediately began drawing up plans for the new temple.

Within a few days men were dispatched into the hills to find wood. Upon their return, the people began rebuilding the temple. But, as the work proceeded, grumbling could be heard among the onlookers: "The new temple sure isn't going to be much to look at!" "Couldn't they have planned a more ornate building?" "Such a drab-looking place!"

God spoke again to Haggai. "Tell the governor and the high priest and all the people these words: 'Some of you remember how beautiful the old temple was—a thing of splendor, a thing of glory. In comparison, the new one is nothing. But do not despair; keep working on it, and in a little while I will overthrow many nations and will bring their treasures here to beautify it. Their gold and their silver and their precious stones are mine, after all. Then the splendor of this temple will be even greater than that of the former one.'

"And tell the people that since the day when they laid the first stone for the foundation of the temple, I have made their fields and their orchards and their vineyards to bring forth abundantly. Now that my people have returned to me, they will eat and be filled, they will have all the clothing they need, and I will remove the holes from the bags in which they bring home their wages."

The Book of Haggai

Theme: God wants his people to be in a right relationship with him.

I. It's time to rebuild the temple (1).

    A. God says the temple should not lie in ruins (1:1-11).

    B. The people agree and begin rebuilding it (1:12-15).

II. The new temple will be glorious (2:1-9).

III. God's people should also be holy and clean (2:10-14).

IV. Then better times will come (2:15-23).

My Dreams
Are Getting Weirder
All the Time

If you think *you've* been having crazy nightmares lately, consider the weird assortment of things that Zechariah the prophet had disturbing his sleep: two women flapping their storklike wings, lugging a lead-lidded crock with a third woman inside it back and forth, back and forth, between heaven and earth; Joshua the priest wandering around in dirty old clothes; four chariots—one pulled by red horses, one by black, one by white, and one by dappled gray—dashing out from between two mountains of bronze.

Mix in a flying scroll, a man with a measuring line, four horns, Satan, and an accumulation of gold lamps, bowls, and pipes, and you have enough to cause even the most stouthearted sleep-

114

er to prefer insomnia, or to make Freud give up in confusion.

Luckily, Zechariah had an interpreter; standing nearby, temporily unemployed, was an angel of the more knowledgeable sort.

"Look," said the angel, "I will explain. To start with, the people you live among have not been on the best terms with God. They have ignored his commands and become pretty rotten—foul, even. God has watched the goings-on long enough. He is angry. He is tired of punishing, tired of giving the back of his hand. So now he makes a new offer: return to him, and he will return to you."

Zechariah weighed and considered the proposal. It was reasonable enough. And more: it was a word from God. So he told the people.

The people listened and realized they had slipped away from God, and many began to walk in his ways again.

A few weeks later a knock came at Zechariah's door, a deputation from the town of Bethel.

"We're wondering," the spokesman began, "which of our old practices we should keep now that we've begun worshiping God again. Particularly we're wondering about this business of fasting. All during the 70 years we were in exile in Babylon, we fasted and mourned during the fifth and seventh months. Should we keep on doing this?"

More rapid than eagles, God's answer came

through Zechariah: "While you were in captivity those 70 years, was it actually for God that you fasted? And when you eat and drink now, do you not do it for yourselves?"

The deputation listened intently.

"God says for you to turn your fast months into feast months. Instead of fasting, show kindness and mercy to each other. Stop oppressing the widow, the fatherless, the visitor, and the poor. Love truth and peace."

"But—" wailed the spokesman for Bethel, "look at how bad the times are!" He wrung his hands symbolically. "Maybe fasting would help!"

"Forget the fasting," Zechariah ordered emphatically, "and turn to God. If you want conditions to be different, be different people. Begin practicing justice and mercy. Try to understand those around you. Be tolerant of those who are different from you. Speak the truth with each other. Fasting is a small matter; if you have truly turned to God, show it in the way you treat each other."

The deputation from Bethel lingered for a few minutes to let Zechariah's words sink in, then set off.

Somehow it was not easy to think of giving up fasting. It had so much to recommend it—the feeling of righteousness pervading one's soul after a whole day without food, the sense of superiority over one's non-fasting brother or sister, the smug assurance that one had obeyed the law to the letter.

Zechariah had not finished prophesying; he still had a message from God about the coming of the Savior:

> The people wander like sheep;
>> they are afflicted for want of a shepherd (10:2).
> Behold, I will bring my servant the Branch (3:8).
> Lo, your king comes to you;
>> triumphant and victorious is he,
>> humble and riding on an ass,
>> on a colt the foal of an ass (9:9).
> When they look on him whom they have pierced,
>> they shall mourn for him (12:10).
> And he shall command peace to the nations;
>> his dominion shall be from sea to sea,
>> and from the River to the ends of the earth (9:10).

The Book of Zechariah

Theme: The Lord controls nature and history.

I. Zechariah calls his people to repentance (1:1-6).

II. Zechariah's visions (1:7—6:8).
    A. The four horsemen (1:8-17).
    B. The four horns and the four smiths (1:18-21).
    C. The angel and the measuring line (2:1-5).
    D. The exiles (2:6-13).
    E. The high priest (3:1-10).
    F. The seven-branched lampstand and the two olive trees (4:1-6a, 10b-14).
    G. Zerubbabel and the temple (4:6b-10a).
    H. The flying scroll (5:1-4).
    I. The woman and the container (5:5-11).
    J. The four chariots (6:1-8).

III. Zerubbabel shall rebuild the temple (6:9-15).

IV. A deputation comes to Zechariah (7-8).
    A. "Shall we fast?" (7:1-3)
    B. "No, rather show kindness and mercy to all" (7:4—8:23).

V. The day of the Lord is coming (9–14).

Shut
the
Church
Doors!

"I wish someone among you would shut the doors of the church and put an end to this farce! Your worship is utter mockery!"

Malachi stood outside the temple and lashed the people with the fury of his words.

"Look at the gifts you bring to God's holy altar!"

The people glanced sheepishly down at the sacrifices they had brought—sickly lambs, corn full of worms, moldy bread.

"Where is your tithe? Have you forgotten that a tenth belongs to your Maker? Will a man rob God? You have!

"And your priests—they don't teach God's

ways. They say, 'What a weariness it is to serve God,' and they sniff at him."

Malachi did not spare the people. Their sins were many, and he proceeded to recount every one of them.

"Look what you have done with marriage, that holy estate which God created to bless you! Intermarrying with the heathen! Unfaithfulness! Violence of every sort!

"And where has your faith dwindled to? You have become so skeptical of God that you say, 'What is the use of living God's way when those who do evil prosper more than we do?' Do you refuse to believe unless you see God's judgment meted out daily upon the disobedient?" Malachi's eyes burned holes in his hearers.

"Do you not know that he loves you, his chosen people? On the last day you will see whether or not it pays to have faith in him. On that day he will be swift against adulterers, against those who speak falsely, against those who oppress their neighbors, against those who have no respect for him."

Thus spoke God through his prophet Malachi, who some have compared with the wise teacher Socrates. Seven times in this short book, Malachi, in a Socratic manner, (1) states a truth, (2) presents objections people raise to that truth, and then (3) gives God's answer to the whole matter.

For instance, this appears in chapter 1, verses 6 and 7:

(1) God says, "A son honors his father, a servant honors his master. I am your father and master, yet you don't honor me, O priests. You despise my name."

(2) "Who? Us?" you say. "When did we ever despise your name?"

(3) God answers: "Every time you say, 'Don't bother bringing anything very valuable to God!'"

But, important as the matters of sacrifice and tithes were to Malachi, he was more concerned about the inward poverty such things indicated in his hearers. The Israelites had forgotten God's divine holiness and majesty. Cut loose from this foundation, they were bewildered, floundering in their relationship to God and in all human relationships as well.

Malachi was sent to arouse the disobedient nation from its spiritual sluggishness and to prepare it for the coming of the long-awaited Savior. To that end God gave him this prophecy to thunder out to the people:

"The Lord will suddenly come to his temple. Then I will draw near to you for judgment. From the days of your fathers you have turned aside from my teachings and have not kept them. Now return to me and I will return to you.

"Return bringing your full tithes into my storehouse, and thereby put me to the test, and see if I will not open the windows of heaven for you and pour down for you an overflowing blessing."

Then God promised that those who had lived

his way would see the end result of their faith: "And I will prepare a book of remembrance of all those who love my name. They shall be mine, my special possession on the day when I judge, and I will spare them as a man spares his son who serves him. Then you will no more be able to say, 'What is the good of our serving God when evil-doers prosper more than we do?'

"For the day is coming when the arrogant and the evildoers shall be as stubble in a burning oven. Neither root nor branch will be left. But for you who fear my name, the Sun of Righteousness shall rise with healing in his wings."

And here, in foretelling the coming of Christ, Malachi ended the message God had given him for the people.

So, to the doubting saints, to the indifferent priests, and to all spiritually careless people, came Malachi's ringing message from God: "Return to me, and I will return to you, and I will open the windows of heaven and pour down for you an overflowing blessing."

Thus ends the last book of the Old Testament, with the windows of heaven ready to open.

The Book of Malachi

Theme: Be faithful to your covenant with the Lord.

  I. God loves his people (1:1-5).

  II. Serve him wholeheartedly (1:6—2:9).

III. Be faithful to him (2:10-16).

IV. God will send his messenger to prepare for the day of judgment (2:17—3:5).

  V. "Return to me," he says, "and I will return to you" (3:6-12).

VI. God's way is the way of life (3:13—4:6).

What Do the Prophets Say to Us Today?

The prophets call us to live as God's people, joyfully and responsibly.

Personal responsibility can easily become blurred in the modern world. Life seems so complex that we sometimes feel ineffectual and helpless, and we can become distracted by many other things. But into this situation the prophets would speak exactly the same message they spoke several thousand years ago: God created and rules over all things. He speaks to us with mercy and love, but also with judgment. Only in him can one find the basis of reality.

The world can be a strange and frightening place, and we can become very tired of hearing

124

about wrongs that need to be righted, but those who are hurting find little rest.

The prophets call us then into a life-giving relationship with our Creator-Redeemer-Sustainer and with fellow human beings. They call us to put aside our false sense of self-sovereignty, our abuse of our freedom, our resentment of God's involvement in our lives. They call us to see where our aggressive, sprawling self-centeredness has led us.

Yet they know God's kingdom is not of this world. They looked forward to the day of the Lord, the day when judgment will be followed by salvation, when all evil will be consumed and the age of eternal fulfillment will begin.

Though the prophets urged God's people to work for justice for all, they knew that full justice will only be realized at the great climax of history, that all human institutions lack the stability to resist their own inner processes of decay. No human institution can produce the good life, for it is beyond the reach of human wisdom and strength.

So the prophets looked forward to the day of the Lord, but they did not try to give any definite idea of when it would come. Today some people think they can date the end of time within a few years. Numerous books have been written, conferences held, and energy spent that might have better been used in doing God's work.

The disciples were also curious about when the

last time would come. They asked Jesus, "Tell us, when will this be, and what will be the sign of your coming and of the close of the age?" (Matt. 24:3).

Jesus answered, "Of that day and hour no one knows, not even the angels in heaven, nor the Son, but the Father only. Watch therefore, for you do not know on what day your Lord is coming. Be ready; for the Son of man is coming at an hour you do not expect" (Matt. 24:36, 42, 44).

He then went on to tell about the master who was going away and set a wise and faithful servant over his household, to see that each person in the household was fed while he was gone. The servant was expected to tend to his master's work, not to waste his time trying to figure out when the master might return. "Blessed is that servant," Jesus said, "whom his master when he comes will find so doing" (Matt. 24:46).

Jesus then told two more stories to illustrate his point. First he told about the five wise and the five foolish maidens and their lamps. The five foolish maidens had not prepared and were not ready to light the bridegroom's way when he came. God gives each of us work to do, Jesus was saying, and we should be doing that work, not trying to guess when he might be coming back.

The second story concerned the man going on a journey who called his three servants and gave to the first, five talents; to the second, two; and to the third, one, expecting that they would put them to work. The first two did, but the third did not. Jesus then told his followers that he was entrusting his work to them: feeding the hungry, clothing the naked, giving drink to the thirsty, visiting the sick and those in prison.

The books of the prophets should not be read therefore as a cryptic plan for the ages that we are to spend our time deciphering, but as God's word to us, calling us from our dead-ended self-centeredness into his kingdom.

The prophets were not God's standup entertainers sent to amuse Israel during slack seasons in the nation's history. Nor were their words spoken to present a tangled skein of yarn to be unsnarled laboriously on the long winter evenings of many centuries, or to provide material for endless debates, or to offer a series of weird images for those who like to dip into the occult and the abstruse. Prophecy is not a parlor game to be played when the TV set breaks down or the news on the radio gets so bizarre that one wonders if indeed the end of the world is immanent.

God has broken into history to speak through individuals, the prophets, culminating in his final revelation in his Son. We may choose to ignore all of these contacts he has made with us. We may choose to look on them as mere diversions from the busy days of our lives. But God is not playing games with us. Through prophecy, God is calling us to be his people. Heaven help us if we look on the prophets' words merely as strange or as being for a different time and people, or as so difficult to understand that we can only put them aside.

The prophets spoke to shine the blazing light of God's justice and righteousness into the dark recesses of society and of human minds.

They spoke to show God's people what life is meant to be and what indeed it can be, when lived in God's presence.

They spoke to call a people back to their God.